THE
YOUNG ADULT'S
GUIDE TO
INVESTING

A Practical Guide to Finance that Helps Young People Plan, Save, and Get Ahead

ROB PIVNICK
Attorney and Financial Advocate

FOR YOUNG READERS

Visit our website at www.skyhorsepublishing.com.

10 9 8 7 6 5 4 3 2

Library of Congress Control Number: 2020930850

Print ISBN: 978-1-63158-537-1
Ebook ISBN: 978-1-63158-538-8

Printed in China

CONTENTS

INTRODUCTION

Have you ever noticed that when you hear one of your friends saying "Wanna bet?" you only hear more about the bet if they won? No one brags if they lose a bet; but we always seem to know when someone wins a bet.

The stock market is pretty much the same. As a teen, you may get a job, earn money from chores or allowance, and maybe eventually go to college. And hopefully you start thinking about investing some of the money you've earned. As you get older you may begin to hear your friends or coworkers brag about how they doubled their money in just one week by buying some particular stock, or generally how they made a bunch of money in the stock market. And then you might think you can do the same—that you can pick a

great stock winner, or that you are smarter than an investment professional whose job it is to manage investments. But don't fool yourself—you will just be gambling, just like anyone who asks "Wanna bet?"

The reality is that no one can beat the market. Anyone thinking they can pick a no-brainer stock winner isn't investing—they are gambling. I didn't want my kids or any other teens falling into the trap of thinking that they can beat the market, so I wrote this book for them and all other readers.

The truth is that no one can consistently beat the market. The professional money managers can't even do it, and they have teams of highly paid and intelligent analysts, as well as powerful computers that run models and algorithms to help them. People may read about some money manager or fund that outpaced the market for a while, maybe even for a few years. But the fact is that only about 15% of them can keep doing it year after year after year. In fact, almost half of all funds end up going out of business because they don't perform. And each of these funds charges its investors a lot of fees/expenses . . . just so they can *underperform*!

Hopefully this book will show readers of all ages that they should invest in certain funds that copy the market (but only those funds that have little or no fees/expenses), as well as not to continuously trade in and out of a stock or fund to chase great returns. Because not only can investors not beat the market, but they can't time the market either. Good investors shouldn't always believe what they read or see in the news about a certain company or investment. If you are investing for the long term, you should just ignore the hype and invest smartly. Generally (unfortunately), we are all terrible investors—and the data proves it. Our best chance for successful investing is to just try to match the market—to just be average.

Investing for the long term is actually pretty simple, if you can tune out all the noise and not think you are smarter than everyone else. I've also included a few life lessons about budgeting and negotiating too, just for good measure. I hope you enjoy this book!

TAKEAWAYS

1. Start saving early; let compounding work wonders for you!

2. Pay credit card debt every month in full.

3. Set goals; make a budget and stick to it.

4. Everything is negotiable.

5. Find out what is important to the other person—ask "why" questions.

6. Invest your money in safe investments if you do not have a lot of time to make your money back or if you need the cash quickly. Take more risk (for higher reward) for longer term savings goals.

7. Invest in indexes; don't be a fool and try to beat the market!

8. Do not try to time the market—you can't! Buy and hold is the best long-term strategy.

9. Do not chase returns!

10. The market always reverts to the mean.

11. Minimize expenses, invest in low-cost index funds.

12. Don't put all your eggs in one basket. Stay diversified and follow a plan.

13. Only hire a professional financial advisor if you really need one—don't automatically assume you should hire one.

14. You are a terrible investor—remember that you can't beat the market. Buy low cost ETFs and ignore all the hype and news.

15. While you should absolutely plan for the future, don't lose sight of the present. Enjoy your life now. It's not all about money.

16. Pursue your passion and curiosity rather than money—odds are you'll end up both happy and financially secure anyway.

CHAPTER 1
SAVINGS

Why Save?

The **experts** say that good saving habits can begin in children as early as three years old . . . so if you are old enough to read this, you are old enough to have some of these habits. Financial skills are one of the most important skills you will need to navigate your life and those skills start with learning to save and budget.

> whoever they are . . .

Unfortunately, at least here in the United States, saving is not a part of most people's behavior. Maybe it's because they did not develop savings habits when they were young—so let's change that.

Why do you need to save money? Because you need money to buy things. Maybe you are saving for a new bike, a new phone, your first car, or just spending money. Maybe you are saving for college. Maybe you are thinking long term and you are saving for your first car, or your first house. Or perhaps you are smart enough to start saving for retirement even though you haven't even gotten your first job. Or maybe you know that you should always have an emergency fund for unexpected costs.

Research has shown that the more you save, the more you want to save. So, build good money habits now and those good habits will stick with you for the rest of your life. Avoid the bad habits that will get you in trouble later.

Global Household Savings Rates

Do yourself a favor and do not follow the lead of most Americans when it comes to saving money. Compared to our neighbors elsewhere around the globe, we save terribly. China and India top the list with a whopping household savings rate around 34%. The global average is 20%. The United States is near the very bottom at 4%. That means, on average, Americans save only 4¢ out of every dollar earned. That's pathetic. Do not be like the average American!

So, how much of every dollar you make should you save? The professionals recommend that you shoot to save between 15–20% of your income. Surely you can at least match the global average.

Compounding

The sooner you start saving, the better off you'll be. Not just because you will have saved more, but because not only are you making money on your initial **investment**, but you'll also be making money on more money. How so? Well, it's called "compounding"—and it is the power of compounding that will make you lots of money. Compounding is when you make money on an investment, and that money is added to the original investment which in turn makes even more money.

Let's look at an example . . . if your rate of **return** is 10% per year on your original investment of $1,000, you make $100 per year. After three years you have a total of $1,300. But let's say that each year you reinvest the $100 you made the prior year. . . after three years you would have $1,331. This is because after the first year, the 10% return applies to $1,100 rather than just $1,000. And the second year, the 10% applies to $1,210. So, the total is $1,331.

investment: money you have put in an account or otherwise used to make more money for yourself

return: the amount you earn on your investment—usually expressed as a percentage

FUN FACT!
The power of compounding was said to be deemed the eighth wonder of the world by Albert Einstein.

An additional $31 might not sound like that much money, but what if we increase the numbers and use a real-life example by comparing two savers: One (let's call him Chris) who starts saving when he is 20 years old and the other (we'll call her Katie) who waits until she

annual: means yearly

is 30 years old. Each one saves $100 per month until they are 60 years old. They both get the same **annual** rate of return of 8.5%.

Chris is smart. He read this book and started saving $100 per month when he was 20 years old and reinvests all earnings. When Chris is 60, he will have an astounding $406,825!

Katie . . . well, she is not so smart. She didn't start saving as early and waited until she was 30 years old. She saves $100 per month and also invests all earnings. When she turns 60, she will only have $166,339.

Chris actually invested only $12,000 more than Katie ($100 per month times ten years) but has accumulated a whopping $240,486 more than Katie! That is the power of compounding. And the earlier you start, the more compounding can work for you. So **start saving now!** Seriously, start now.

DID YOU KNOW?

*A **401K** is a savings plan set up by an employer for the benefit of its employees. In many cases, the employer will match a portion of the money the employee saves! So if you ever work for a company that offers a matching contribution to a 401K, make sure you take advantage of the matching amount the employer gives. It's free money!*

More on both of these types of accounts in Chapter 7

*An **IRA** is a retirement account that is similar to a 401K, but it isn't through your employer–you can set it up yourself. It provides tax savings that might enable your money to increase tax free. As soon as you have a job and earn "taxable income" you can set up an IRA. And remember: the earlier the better. Free money!*

FUN FACT!

The "Rule of 72" is a quick method to determine how long it will take for you to double your money. You simply divide the return rate into 72. The result is the approximate number of years that it will take for your investment to double. Similarly, if you flip it by dividing the number of years within which you want to double your money into 72, the result is the approximate return you'll need to earn to do so. For example, if you want to know how long it will take to double your money at 8% interest, divide 8 into 72 . . . the answer is 9 years.

TAKEAWAY #1:
Start saving early; let compounding work wonders for you!

CHAPTER 2

BUDGETING, DEBT, AND SETTING GOALS

Federal Debt and Deficit

deficit:
the amount that spending exceeds income

In another example of do-not-follow-the-lead-of-most-Americans (or at least certainly not our federal government), the total amount of debt that the United States government owes is over $22 trillion. That's $22,000,000,000,000. And in recent years our government has run a **deficit** of anywhere between $438 billion and $1.4 trillion per year. If you want to see the zeroes . . . that's between $438,000,000,000 and $1,400,000,000,000. In fact, the last year our federal government made more money than it spent was in 2001.

surplus:
the opposite of deficit; it occurs when more money is earned than is spent

Even as you read this you know that you may have to wait before you can buy something you want because you don't have the money. There is a difference between things you want and things you need.

Consumer Debt

American consumers owe more than $1 trillion in credit card debt. There is an additional $1.5 trillion in student loan debt outstanding. And just over three quarters of a million people filed for **bankruptcy** in 2019 (the most recent year data is available). Even though the experts say that the concept of "wants" versus "needs" can be understood by children between ages of 3 and 5, it seems pretty clear that plenty of adults don't know much about budgeting.

bankruptcy:
a legal procedure for those who have spent way too much money and have to go to a judge because they cannot repay their debts—it makes it hard for anyone to trust you or let you borrow money afterwards

DID YOU KNOW?

As a general rule you should try to avoid borrowing money, but certain types of debt are okay. The $1.5 trillion in outstanding student loan debt is not necessarily a bad thing. Debt for additional education is money well spent as people who have college and graduate degrees earn much more than people who do not—consider this:

- *Those with a college degree earn on average 57% more than people with only a high school diploma; and*
- *People with graduate degrees earn an additional 27% more on average than those with only a college degree.*

Similarly, debt for things you might "need" as opposed to things you just "want" makes sense also. For example, borrowing money to buy your first house isn't bad; borrowing to purchase a car may be okay; and borrowing money to start a business likely makes good sense. It's debt for the "wants" that you should stay away from. And make sure you pay your credit card bills in full every month—that is a great habit (especially because some banks charge credit card users 29% interest or more if not paid).

mortgage:
a loan on a home

Budgeting

We all have to make choices about how to spend our money. This is called budgeting. A budget sets forth your anticipated income and spending over a period of time. It allows you to see what you can afford, how much you can spend, and if you need to cut back on buying things because you don't (or won't) have enough money.

There is simply not enough money to buy everything you might want. You have to **prioritize**. You may have to wait to buy something you want because you can't afford it or because you need something else. Avoid becoming one of the adults who does not understand this concept—

prioritize: to decide what is most important

make a budget and set goals. Compare how much you make in allowance, how much you make from chores or your job, and how much you have in savings against how much you can spend and how much you want to save.

Write down these amounts so you know how much you can really spend on the things you need and want. Please note: Make sure your budget takes into consideration the 20% savings goal you have set for yourself.

You can be a smarter consumer than most of the adults with all that credit card debt! Before you buy something expensive, research it, shop around, compare prices, and ask questions. Do you really need the item, or can you live without it? Are you replacing something broken? Do you have something else that will work just as well? What advantages does the new one offer?

TAKEAWAY #2:
Pay credit card debt every month in full.

Once you have made your budget you can then set goals for what you are saving your money for. In fact, studies have shown that people who actually write down their goals on a piece of paper are actually 33% more likely to reach them, so jot down your goals—perhaps on the same paper you did your budget. Stick it on your mirror, put it on your nightstand, or keep it in your underwear drawer! And if you have to make an unexpected purchase, or decide you just have to have that new phone, you can look at your budget and see what other purchases you would have to cut out to do so . . . then you can make a smart decision about it.

TAKEAWAY #3:
Set goals; make a budget and stick to it.

CHAPTER 3
NEGOTIATION AND MAKING DEALS

No discussion about saving and budgeting would be complete without addressing negotiation. You will never save money quicker than when you are negotiating with someone. Usually, all you have to do is ask for a discount and you may get it.

So how can you use negotiating to save you money, and how should you go about negotiating with people? First off, remember: everything is negotiable. And even if it is not, it never hurts to ask because the worst they can say is "no."

Tips/Techniques

1. **Small Talk** – One of the most important things you can do at the beginning of (or even before you start) a negotiation is get to know the other person. Even one minute of small talk about their favorite team, where they grew up, what their interests are, etc. will serve you well. This is because people want to help out others that they like. Showing an interest in someone lets them know you care about them and that you're likeable. Plus, you might find something out about them that you both have in common. This is important because people are also more likely to help others that are similar to them. Studies have shown that engaging in small talk results in more successful negotiations. Small talk = big gains.

2. **Be Friendly** – When you think of negotiating with someone or making a better deal, you may think that you're on the opposite side as they are. But this "opposite side" mentality will only hurt you. You will get better results if people like you, so be friendly.

3. **Silence** – People generally are uncomfortable in a conversation in which there is total silence. So, ask for whatever discount you want then keep your trap shut! If you don't say anything, odds are that the other person will end up giving you some sort of discount. If they offer you a discount don't immediately reply; stay silent—they may break the silence with an even bigger discount!

4. **What is Motivating Them?** – In order to be a successful negotiator, you must find out what the other person's interests are. What is important to them? How will the result affect them? If you don't know what they want, you won't be able to get what is best for both of you. Here is a quick story that should show you that *you must ask questions* when you're negotiating:

> *Two brothers were in the kitchen fighting over the last orange. "I need the orange." "No, I want the orange!" So, they grabbed a kitchen knife and cut the orange in half. This seems fair, right? Fair, yes, but not the best solution. You see, one brother needed the orange to make fresh squeezed juice. The other one only needed the peel for his favorite cake. But because they cut it in half, the first brother had just half a cup of fresh squeezed juice; the other didn't have enough peel for his recipe. They both ended up "losing." Had they simply asked each other WHY they wanted the orange, they each would have gotten exactly what they wanted. It would have been a win-win situation.*

5. **Ask for the Moon** – It may sound unreasonable to ask for a huge discount if you only want the price knocked down a little bit. But it is really the smartest thing you can do. Here's why:
    a. You might actually end up getting it!
    b. It leaves room to negotiate from the outrageous position to what you really want.

Information is King

Information is the most important thing in a negotiation. The person who has the most complete information has the edge. That is why, as you see from number 4 above, you must ask questions to find out what the other person's interests are. You must ask "why" questions.

> **DID YOU KNOW?**
> *A person's interest is different from their position. In the orange story above, each brother's position was "I want the orange." But their interests were quite different—one wanted the juice, the other wanted the peel. So, to be a successful negotiator, you must find out what the other person's interests are.*
>
> *Next time your little brother or sister is whining about something, ask questions to find out what exactly they are upset about, it might not be what you (or even they) think!*

Asking questions gets you information. If you are just buying a product, however, the most important information you might need is how that product is being offered at competitors' stores. How is it priced online? Are others offering rebates? Free delivery? Extended warranties? Free repairs? If you comparison shop all these things before you decide to make your final purchase, you should easily be able to negotiate your final sale to get the best deal you can.

And remember, you will never save money quicker than when you are negotiating with someone.

TAKEAWAY #4:
Everything is negotiable.

TAKEAWAY #5:
Find out what is important to the other person—ask "why" questions.

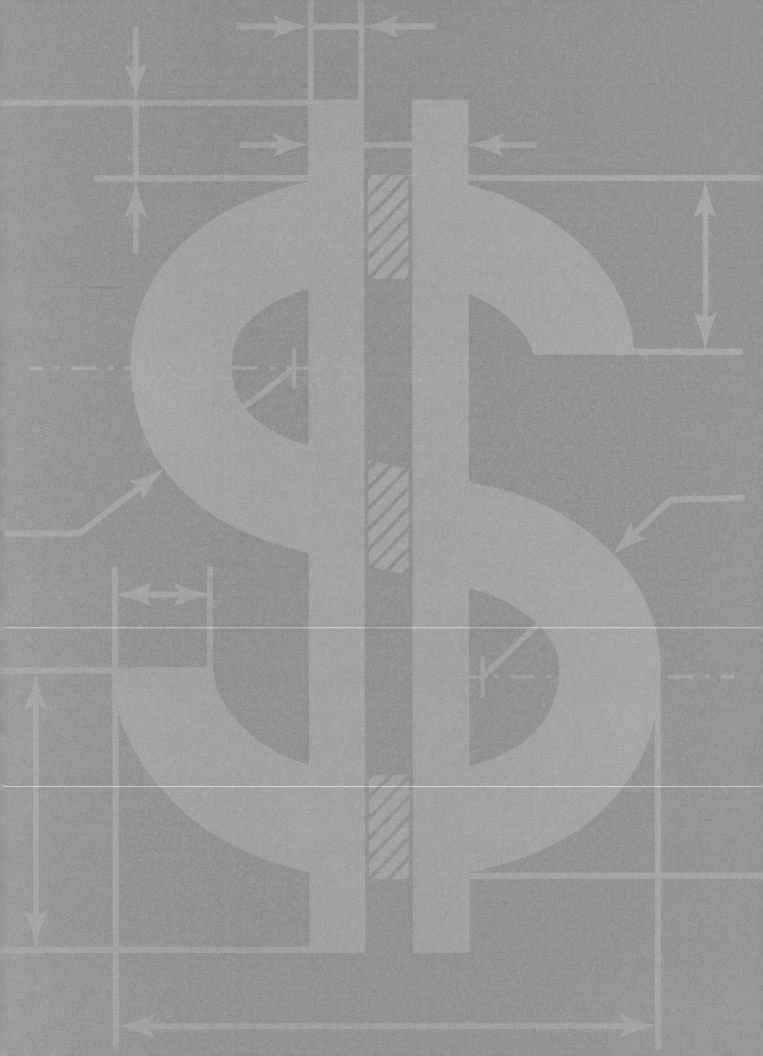

CHAPTER 4

RISK V. REWARD

How Much Risk Should You Take?

Now, back to saving . . . The type of investment you put your money into depends on how much risk you are willing to take. As a general rule in investments (and in life), you cannot expect to achieve higher reward without taking more risk. The chart below offers a very basic look at this relationship.

The investments on the bottom left offer the **least opportunity for reward** but they are the safest investments. Those on the top right have the potential for much higher returns, but this comes at a **much-increased risk**.

meaning their returns are low

that is, the increased possibility that you could lose all your money

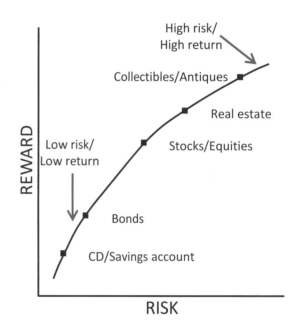

For example, bank savings accounts and certificates of deposits (CDs) offer very, very low returns close to 0.1%, but these savings vehicles are insured by our federal government if they are with one of the many banks you customarily see in your neighborhood. If you've seen the FDIC sticker below on the door of your bank, then your money is guaranteed by the United States government up to $250,000—meaning that if your particular bank ever went out of business, the government would give you your money.

DID YOU KNOW?

The FDIC was created in 1933 near the end of the Great Depression to create a sense of comfort and confidence in the American people that any money they had in member banks was guaranteed by the government, even if the bank failed. This was meant to prevent people from panicking and taking all their money out of the bank and avoid a "run on the banks."

Because **stocks** are riskier investments than savings in a FDIC member bank, if you invest in equities you should expect to earn a higher return. And this is the case—historical equity returns have averaged around 8.5% per year. And because investing in collectibles, such as jewels, antiques, coins, baseball cards, cars, or even wine, is much riskier, the potential returns for those investments must be even higher than stocks—to compensate for the higher risk. But the risk of losing your money in these investments is also much greater.

So, all this leads to the question of which investment is the "right" investment? You must consider all sorts of things when figuring out your risk tolerance. Your risk tolerance determines your willingness to benefit from an incredible investment at the possibility of losing your money. Take too little risk, and you won't make as much money; take too much risk, and you could lose all your money. Several factors play into this decision:

1. Would you risk losing most of your money in the short term, for the possibility of amazing returns in the long term?
2. What is your investment horizon—that is, how soon do you need the money?
3. Will you need **access to your money quickly** in the future?
4. Can you change your plans? Do you have the ability to alter what you would use the money for if the investment goes poorly?

Investment Horizon

Your investment horizon is the amount of time you plan to hold onto your investment. The longer the horizon, the greater your ability to take more risk for higher reward. Long term investments allow you to recover from a bad year or two (or three or more) and benefit from potential higher returns. But if your horizon is very short, stick to safe investments so you don't risk losing any money before you need it.

Liquidity

How much cash will you need to get quickly? If you need to access cash quickly for school supplies, new shoes, clothes, or a new phone, funds for those expenses should be in investments that are quickly able to be used.

Asset Allocation

"Asset allocation" determines which investments you choose depending on how old you are, where you are in life, and when you'll need your money. It is how you divide your money into different asset classes. It's a fancy way to describe where you stash your money, depending on when you might need it.

Asset Classes

You invest by balancing risk and reward depending on your own goals, risk tolerance, and investment horizon. The three main asset classes that are discussed in this book are stocks, bonds and cash. They have different levels of risk and return, so each will behave differently over time.

- **Equities** (sometimes called stocks) are ownership interests in a company or an asset. These have the potential to make or lose a lot of money, so both the risk and reward are high. Equities are investments you should hold for longer investment horizon. You can buy stock in companies like Nike, McDonald's, AT&T, and Coca-Cola, plus many other smaller companies you have never heard of.
- **Bonds** (fixed income or debt instruments) are investments in which you loan money to a company. You are a lender (sometimes called a creditor) rather than an owner. Bonds are generally safer investments than equity which means that the potential returns should be lower. You can **buy bonds** in companies like Nike, McDonald's, AT&T, and Coca-Cola. You can also actually lend money to the United States government (and lots of other countries) and its states and cities. Recall from Chapter 2 that the United States government has borrowed approximately $22 trillion.

  > **buy bonds:** in other words, loan money to

- **Cash** is simply the money you have in your checking or savings account (or stashed under your mattress!) that you can access immediately. The bank isn't paying you much (if any) interest, so there is not much reward in keeping money in the bank, but it is the safest place to put it so you will always know it will be there.

The process of determining which mix of assets works for you today depends on the factors described above. And your risk tolerance today is not the same as it will be later in your life.

TAKEAWAY #6:

Invest your money in safe investments if you do not have a lot of time to make your money back or if you need the cash quickly. Take more risk (for higher reward) for longer term savings goals.

> *Note that most of the remainder of this book is geared towards longer term investment choices, because if you need your money very quickly, your investment choices are pretty limited.*

CHAPTER 5
ACTIVE V. PASSIVE—WHICH IS BETTER?

> **Y**ou should be happy with average! It is better to be the market than to beat the market. It isn't very often in life that you don't want to be better than most ... But at the end of this chapter, you should *want to be average when it comes to investing!*

Adopt a Low-Cost Strategy—Minimize Expenses

The next three chapters may not be the most exciting part of the book, but they might just be the most important, so ... stay with me here.

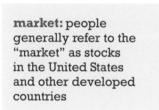

market: people generally refer to the "market" as stocks in the United States and other developed countries

Historically, **market** returns have averaged around 8.5% annually. So, as you saw from the compounding example in Chapter 1, this book will use 8.5% as a historical return average. That does *not* mean that in any given year returns won't be better or worse, but over the long term, 8.5% is the approximate average.

Active

All investors have a choice of investment style when trying to achieve or beat that return average: active or passive. "Active investing" is a strategy in which an investment fund (or fund manager) attempts to outperform the market; the goal of active management is to beat the market or a particular **benchmark**. This strategy is for those that think they're smarter than everyone else.

benchmark: a standard used to measure the performance of an investment— more on that below

Passive/Indexes

"Passive management," or "indexing," is an investment approach in which the fund's goal is to match the performance of the market (or match a particular sector, industry, or region within the market as a whole) as closely as possible, rather than try to beat it. Indexing does this by investing in the same securities in the same proportions as a market or sector. There are thousands of index funds available that track particular markets, sectors, industries or regions. Indexes represent benchmarks. Examples of indexes that you see on TV or online are:

- Dow Jones Industrial Average (representing 30 of the largest and most well-known companies in the United States)
- Standard & Poor's (S&P) 500 (representing the 500 largest companies in the United States)
- Russell 2000 (representing the smallest companies in America)
- Nasdaq Composite (following companies listed on the Nasdaq, which is tilted towards technological companies)
- Wilshire 5000 (this is a total market index of the United States including all companies)
- EAFE (representing international markets "Europe Australasia and the Far East")

DID YOU KNOW?

The first index, and the one that is commonly referred to when someone in America asks, "How did the market do today?", was created by Charles Dow in 1896. It has evolved into what we know today as the Dow Jones Industrial Average.

This book aims to convince you that you should follow a passive investment strategy. The professionals advise investors that it is impossible to consistently beat the market without increasing risk. This idea is called the "efficient market hypothesis"—it states that the market itself is efficient and its performance is based on all the information about stocks that is available, so beating the market without taking on more risk is impossible. Some studies have shown that there are some **anomalies** in the market that might allow for opportunities to beat the market over the short term—but over the long term the markets are efficient.

anomalies: things that are different from what is normal or expected

The word "consistently" above is emphasized because that is the key point. For any given period, or even for a day, someone can pick a stock that will beat the market . . . but that person will have to do that day after day after day, year after year after year, to actually come out on top. One trade, one day, or one year even does not make someone a successful investor.

FUN FACT!

The efficient market hypothesis is like another (more fun) theory of market performance—the "random walk," which states that the markets change according to a random walk and cannot be predicted.

Burton Malkiel (a Princeton University professor) took this a step further and argued that a blindfolded monkey throwing darts at a newspaper's stock pages could select a portfolio that would do just as well as one selected by pros. The Wall Street Journal (the primary business newspaper in the United States) ran a competition to see if darts thrown at random stocks could actually beat the professionals. Their conclusion: it was essentially a tie.

DID YOU KNOW?

*In 1974, the late, great John "Jack" Bogle founded the Vanguard Group, which is the largest **mutual fund** company in the world. He took the stance that "if you can't beat 'em, join 'em" and one year later created the first low-cost index **ETF** mirroring the S&P 500 index.*

Jack is one of the smartest investors of our time.

Even Warren Buffett (of Berkshire Hathaway), who is one of the wealthiest people in the world and may actually be the greatest investor we may ever know, says that most investors should follow an indexing strategy.

mutual fund: pools money from many investors in a professionally managed investment portfolio of stocks, bonds, or other assets

ETFs (or "exchange traded funds") are similar to mutual funds, but they can be traded throughout the day like stocks and track the returns of any number of indexes, sectors, or markets

The chart below shows how passive index funds beat actively managed funds over a five-year period (this chart shows the five years ended 2017, but the results would be similar for nearly any five-year period). The percentages show how many actively managed funds beat the benchmark for their category. And, by the way, these results show all funds, even those that closed within the time period. (Their results may have been so bad that they went out of business—too bad for the people who thought they were actually smarter than the market and invested in those funds.)

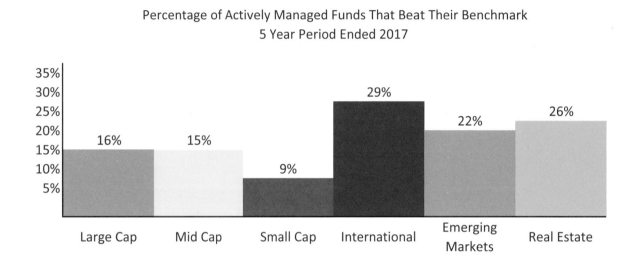

Percentage of Actively Managed Funds That Beat Their Benchmark
5 Year Period Ended 2017

The exact stats vary depending on the year and type of asset category, but on average, anywhere from 70–90% of funds *cannot* beat the market. Only 10–30% of professionals beat the market year after year.

TAKEAWAY #7:
Invest in indexes; don't be a fool and try to beat the market!

Do Not Try to Time the Market

A passive investment approach necessarily means that you should **not try to time the market** either. Many people might try to convince you that you can get into the market in good times . . . and get out before the bad times . . . then get back in before the next upswing. They will say that staying invested all the time should not be followed. The first decade of the 2000s had a lot of ups and downs, so it is not a surprise that some people do not favor a buy-and-hold strategy. But the question you have to ask yourself is "Do you think you're

this is called a "buy-and-hold" strategy

smart enough to time the market's movements?" The answer is . . . no. If you are a long-term investor, you should not try to time the market.

In fact, most investors miss out on the good times precisely because they jump in and out of the market at the wrong times because they think they can time it. In the 20-year period ended in 2017, stock investors earned only 5% a year due to terrible market timing, nearly 4 percentage points less than a buy-and-hold strategy (and the market historical average).

But what if you could avoid the bad days? If you thought you could time the market and miss all the bad days, you'd be in great shape. But if you get out of the market at the wrong times, you also end up missing out on big rallies. If you missed out on *just the 10 best days* in the same 20-year period, your average annual return would have dropped to 3.5%. Miss the 30 best days and would have lost money.

It is virtually impossible for investors to successfully predict the market in order to capture good performance and avoid bad performance. Remember, the professionals whose job it is

commissions: fees that are charged to investors every time they buy or sell

to do this and who get paid based on their success cannot do it 70–90% of the time! Why would you think you can do it? To be sure though, if you think you are smarter than the market and all those professionals, at least know what you are up against and make a reasoned decision to be an active investor. And don't forget . . . trading in and out costs **commissions** that lower your returns even more.

DID YOU KNOW?

There is a method that allows investors to time the market (sort of) to reduce downside risk. It is called

In the United Kingdom, this is called "pound cost averaging"

"dollar cost averaging." An investor "averages" his or her purchases into the market by investing the same amount of money following a set schedule. This way, he or she buys fewer shares when the stock price is higher, and when it is lower, he or she buys more shares. It's like buying when the stock is on sale! Dollar cost averaging reduces the average share cost and lowers downside risk.

For example, let's say you decide to purchase $100 worth of Widget Co. stock each month for three months. In the first month, Widget Co. is worth $33, so you buy three shares. In the second month, Widget Co. is worth $25, so you buy four additional shares. Finally, in the third month, Widget Co. is worth $20, so you buy five shares. In total, you purchased 12 shares for an average price of $25 each. Dollar cost averaging has the effect of lowering the overall average cost per share paid.

TAKEAWAY #8:
Do not try to time the market—you can't!
Buy and hold is the best long-term strategy.

Do Not Chase Returns—Stay the Diversified Course

A passive investment style necessarily means that as an investor you do not **chase returns**. You should not expect that an investment's past performance from last year will continue the next year. In fact, most stocks and funds that beat the market in the past generally will not do so in the future. Good past performance is often a matter of luck. This is why active investors who constantly chase returns get burned. Why? Because past performance is not an indication of future performance and cannot guarantee future results.

> **chase returns:** always investing in the latest great investment

The following chart shows how past returns simply do not predict future results; it shows the main asset types over a fifteen-year period, and how the market changes every year. Notice that the performance of any type of investment changes just about every year. So, if you picked the hot investment one year (pick a color, any color . . .), you might find that investment is the worst the next year.

2004	2005	2006	2007	2008	2009	2010	2011	2012	2013	2014	2015	2016	2017	2018
MSCI EMERGING MARKETS 25.95%	MSCI EMERGING MARKETS 34.54%	MSCI EMERGING MARKETS 32.59%	MSCI EMERGING MARKETS 39.78%	BARCLAYS AGG BOND 5.24%	MSCI EMERGING MARKETS 79.02%	RUSSELL 2000 GROWTH 29.09%	BARCLAYS AGG BOND 7.84%	MSCI EMERGING MARKETS 18.63%	RUSSELL 2000 GROWTH 43.30%	S&P 500 GROWTH 14.67%	S&P 500 GROWTH 5.33%	RUSSELL 2000 VALUE 31.74%	MSCI EMERGING MARKETS 37.28%	BARCLAYS AGG BOND 0.01%
RUSSELL 2000 VALUE 22.25%	MSCI EAFE 13.54%	MSCI EAFE 26.34%	MSCI EAFE 11.17%	BARCLAYS CORP. HIGH YIELD -26.16%	BARCLAYS CORP. HIGH YIELD 58.21%	RUSSELL 2000 26.85%	BARCLAYS CORP. HIGH YIELD 4.98%	RUSSELL 2000 VALUE 18.05%	RUSSELL 2000 38.82%	S&P 500 13.70%	S&P 500 1.38%	RUSSELL 2000 21.31%	S&P 500 GROWTH 27.20%	S&P 500 GROWTH -0.17%
MSCI EAFE 20.25%	S&P 500 VALUE 5.82%	RUSSELL 2000 VALUE 23.48%	S&P 500 GROWTH 9.13%	RUSSELL 2000 VALUE -28.92%	RUSSELL 2000 GROWTH 34.47%	RUSSELL 2000 VALUE 24.50%	S&P 500 GROWTH 4.65%	S&P 500 VALUE 17.68%	RUSSELL 2000 VALUE 34.52%	S&P 500 VALUE 12.14%	BARCLAYS AGG BOND 0.55%	S&P 500 VALUE 17.17%	MSCI EAFE 25.03%	BARCLAYS CORP. HIGH YIELD -3.18%
RUSSELL 2000 18.33%	S&P 500 4.91%	S&P 500 VALUE 20.81%	RUSSELL 2000 GROWTH 7.05%	RUSSELL 2000 -33.79%	MSCI EAFE 31.78%	MSCI EMERGING MARKETS 19.20%	S&P 500 2.11%	MSCI EAFE 17.32%	S&P 500 GROWTH 32.75%	BARCLAYS AGG BOND 5.97%	MSCI EAFE -0.81%	BARCLAYS CORP. HIGH YIELD 14.75%	RUSSELL 2000 GROWTH 22.17%	S&P 500 -4.38%
S&P 500 VALUE 15.71%	RUSSELL 2000 VALUE 4.71%	RUSSELL 2000 18.37%	BARCLAYS AGG BOND 6.97%	S&P 500 GROWTH -34.92%	S&P 500 GROWTH 31.57%	BARCLAYS CORP. HIGH YIELD 15.12%	S&P 500 VALUE -0.48%	RUSSELL 2000 16.35%	S&P 500 32.39%	RUSSELL 2000 GROWTH 5.60%	RUSSELL 2000 GROWTH -1.38%	S&P 500 11.96%	S&P 500 21.83%	RUSSELL 2000 GROWTH -9.31%
RUSSELL 2000 GROWTH 14.31%	RUSSELL 2000 4.55%	S&P 500 15.79%	S&P 500 5.49%	S&P 500 -37.00%	RUSSELL 2000 27.17%	S&P 500 VALUE 15.10%	RUSSELL 2000 GROWTH -2.91%	S&P 500 14.61%	S&P 500 VALUE 31.99%	RUSSELL 2000 4.90%	S&P 500 VALUE -3.24%	RUSSELL 2000 GROWTH 11.32%	S&P 500 VALUE 15.19%	S&P 500 VALUE -9.09%
BARCLAYS CORP. HIGH YIELD 11.13%	RUSSELL 2000 GROWTH 4.15%	RUSSELL 2000 GROWTH 13.35%	S&P 500 VALUE 1.99%	RUSSELL 2000 GROWTH -38.54%	S&P 500 26.47%	S&P 500 15.06%	RUSSELL 2000 -4.18%	BARCLAYS CORP. HIGH YIELD 15.81%	MSCI EAFE 22.78%	RUSSELL 2000 VALUE 4.22%	RUSSELL 2000 -4.41%	MSCI EMERGING MARKETS 11.19%	RUSSELL 2000 14.65%	RUSSELL 2000 -11.01%
S&P 500 10.88%	S&P 500 GROWTH 4.00%	BARCLAYS CORP. HIGH YIELD 11.85%	BARCLAYS CORP. HIGH YIELD 1.87%	S&P 500 VALUE -39.22%	S&P 500 VALUE 21.17%	S&P 500 GROWTH 15.05%	RUSSELL 2000 VALUE -5.50%	S&P 500 GROWTH 14.61%	BARCLAYS CORP. HIGH YIELD 7.44%	BARCLAYS CORP. HIGH YIELD 1.15%	BARCLAYS CORP. HIGH YIELD -7.22%	S&P 500 GROWTH 6.74%	RUSSELL 2000 VALUE 7.84%	RUSSELL 2000 VALUE -12.86%
S&P 500 GROWTH 6.13%	BARCLAYS CORP. HIGH YIELD 2.74%	S&P 500 GROWTH 11.01%	RUSSELL 2000 -1.57%	MSCI EAFE -43.38%	RUSSELL 2000 VALUE 20.58%	MSCI EAFE 7.75%	MSCI EAFE -12.14%	RUSSELL 2000 GROWTH 14.59%	BARCLAYS AGG BOND -2.02%	MSCI EMERGING MARKETS -2.19%	RUSSELL 2000 VALUE -7.47%	BARCLAYS AGG BOND 2.65%	BARCLAYS CORP. HIGH YIELD 6.48%	MSCI EAFE -13.79%
BARCLAYS AGG BOND 4.34%	BARCLAYS AGG BOND 2.43%	BARCLAYS AGG BOND 4.33%	RUSSELL 2000 VALUE -9.78%	MSCI EMERGING MARKETS -53.18%	BARCLAYS AGG BOND 5.93%	BARCLAYS AGG BOND 6.54%	MSCI EMERGING MARKETS -18.17%	BARCLAYS AGG BOND 4.21%	MSCI EMERGING MARKETS -2.27%	MSCI EAFE -4.90%	MSCI EMERGING MARKETS -14.92%	MSCI EAFE 1.00%	BARCLAYS AGG BOND 3.54%	MSCI EMERGING MARKETS -14.58%

But believe it or not, studies have shown that past returns is the primary investment decision most investors consider when choosing among investments! But of course, hopefully you know by now that you cannot time the market and that active investing is not the way to go.

TAKEAWAY #9:
Do not chase returns!

TAKEAWAY #10:
The market always reverts to the mean.

Minimize Costs/Expenses

Hopefully you are convinced that trying to beat the market is a fool's game. So, let's take it a step further and boost returns even more. We do this by eliminating or reducing fees that funds charge.

In life, people like to say that "you get what you pay for." This does NOT apply to investing! Lower-cost funds actually outperform higher-cost funds. Every dollar paid for management fees or trading commissions is simply a dollar wasted.

The chart below shows how fees and expenses affect investment returns. The chart shows thirty-years' growth of $100,000 assuming an 8.5% annual return. The black line shows returns for paying no fees at all; the blue line shows low cost funds that only charge 0.25% expenses (which is about average for passive funds); and the red line shows a higher expense ratio of 1.25% (this is also about average expense costs for actively managed funds). You would have wasted almost $280,000

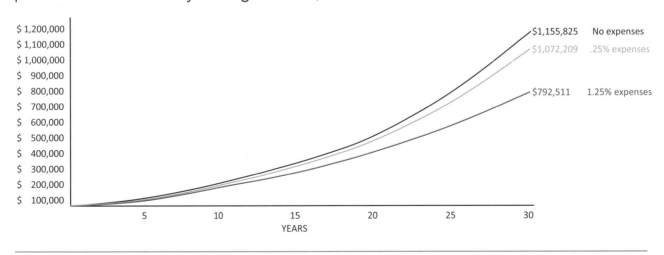

by investing in funds with higher costs as opposed to the low-cost index funds!! So, you can increase your return by beating the market, if you think you can. Or you can lower your costs. . . . You decide which is easier. Do you have the skills to beat the market when far less than half of the professionals cannot do it over the long term (remember the blindfolded monkeys)?

Actively managed funds eventually revert to the mean but charge much higher fees. Index funds charge much lower fees than actively managed funds, and they too provide market average returns. So, if all investments ultimately produce the same returns, why would you pay much more for the actively managed funds? Indexing/passive investing will make you more money because it provides the same returns as active investing at a much, much lower cost.

Higher Fees Do Not Mean Better Performance!

One final chart to hammer home the point that you do not always get what you pay for. The red bars represent the highest cost funds and the blue bars represent the lowest cost funds for various asset classes for the ten-year period ended 2017. In every category, the low-cost fund outperformed the high-cost fund!

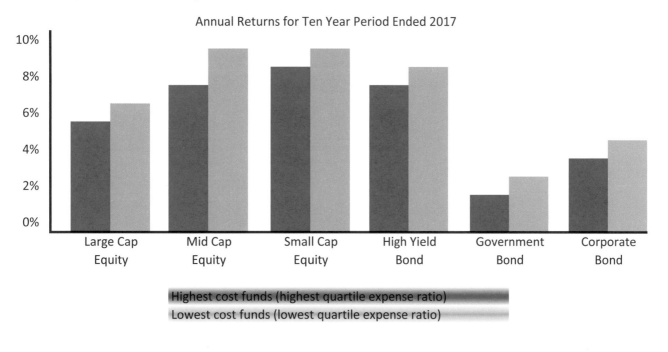

Annual Returns for Ten Year Period Ended 2017

Highest cost funds (highest quartile expense ratio)
Lowest cost funds (lowest quartile expense ratio)

TAKEAWAY #11:
Minimize expenses, invest in low-cost index funds.

A Note on Inflation

Inflation is the rate at which things get more expensive every year. The historical average rate of inflation in the United States is around 3% per year. It is measured by the Consumer Price Index which is a pretend basket of goods and services that the U.S. government publishes to represent the items that the general public purchases and uses.

deflation: the opposite of inflation—it's when prices go down

Why do you care about inflation? You care because the new phone that you want this year will be more expensive next year. And the money you have saved right now will be worth less next year—in terms of how much it can purchase. Inflation eats into the annual return you earn on your investments. If you look at the growth of $100,000 over thirty years shown on the first chart under the "Minimize Costs/Expenses" topic shown earlier—the low-cost index strategy grew to $1,072,209. But when inflation is factored, it is really worth only an inflation-adjusted $441,766. Inflation "cost" $630,443 in purchasing power!

If you've ever heard one of your grandparents say, "I remember when I could go to a movie for 25¢ and a soda cost a nickel . . .", well, that's inflation.

So, is inflation bad? Not really. Inflation actually has the effect of eroding debt (it's the reverse of the savings example above where inflation hurts)—it effectively "lowers" the amount borrowers have to pay back in inflation-adjusted terms. Also, inflation boosts **wages**, so that's good. A little bit of inflation keeps our economy humming along.

wages: the amount people get paid to work

High inflation, however, claws away at savings, as shown above, makes monthly bills go up, and effectively lowers wages (because the amount people are paid does not go up as much as the price of goods during high inflation).

So, if high inflation is bad, does that mean deflation is

good? No . . . quite the opposite. Would you buy that scooter today for $800 if you knew that it would only cost you (and only be worth) $700 in a few weeks? You'd probably wait, right? Well, in a few weeks, why not wait a bit longer when it will only cost $600?

You see that deflation makes consumers less willing to spend money. But people buying things is what keeps our economy going—if people stop buying, our economy grinds to a halt. This results in people losing their jobs too. Then you could forget about a historic average of 8.5% returns . . . no, those returns would turn negative.

CHAPTER 6
DIVERSIFICATION

Now that you are hopefully convinced that you *absolutely should* (1) start saving early, (2) use index funds, (3) try not to beat the market—but be satisfied matching the market, (4) try not to time the market or chase returns, but invest for the long term, and (5) minimize costs. How do you put all this together? Well, let's look at the types of investments you might consider and how to build your portfolio for the long term.

Does low risk always mean lower returns? And, to increase returns, do you have to take more risk? There actually is a way you can achieve higher returns without taking on more risk: by **diversifying** your investments! Diversification allows an investor to lower risk without lowering the expected return.

diversifying: spreading out your money over different types of investments

By combining different types of investments in a smart way, you spread out your investment over a wide variety of sectors and asset classes. The risk that any specific investment will fail is partially canceled by all other investments and overall risk is lowered. Diversification differs from asset allocation in that when you diversify, you choose different sectors or types of investments within a particular asset class (say, for example, equities), as opposed to asset allocation which is spreading your investment over asset types with different risk (e.g., equities, bonds, and cash).

Having a diversified portfolio invested in a variety of stocks and a variety of sectors lowers the risk of losing much money when one particular investment declines. Too bad diversification cannot protect against risk that the entire market and economy may have a bad year (or more).

FUN FACT!

Two crazy smart guys named Harry Markowitz and Bill Sharpe basically invented the modern diversified "portfolio" theory of investing in 1952. They even created a graph showing the "efficient frontier" to prove that diversification can lower risk without lowering returns. Anywhere on this line represents an efficient portfolio; anywhere below it is a portfolio that needs work!

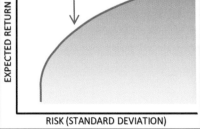

I don't really get it either, but now you've seen the "efficient frontier"

Building a Diversified Portfolio

The most basic method of diversification is to buy a mutual fund or index fund instead of the stock of just one company. Mutual funds could own shares in twenty, thirty, forty, or hundreds of companies giving you instant diversification. But, how can we diversify in an even better way to increase returns without increasing risk? Below is just one example of a properly diversified portfolio that you may consider. Before we start, though, let's learn one more definition: "standard deviation." It's sort of confusing, but let's just say that standard deviation is a measurement of risk that shows how much the returns of an investment stray from the average. The lower the number, the more consistent the returns and less risk; the higher the number the more variance and more risk.

Step One: Basic Portfolio

Start out with just two investments: 60% in equities (S&P 500 Index) and 40% in government bonds (Barclay's Government Credit Index). The average annual return over the 40+ years shown was 8.8%; the standard deviation (risk) was 11.3%.

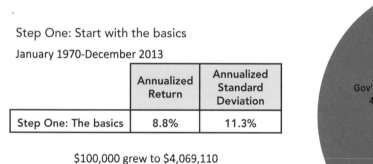

Step One: Start with the basics

January 1970-December 2013

	Annualized Return	Annualized Standard Deviation
Step One: The basics	8.8%	11.3%

$100,000 grew to $4,069,110

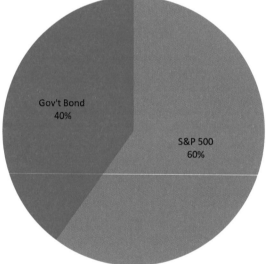

Step Two: Adjust Bonds

On the bond side, the experts who designed this portfolio use government bonds only: 50% intermediate-term, 30% short-term and 20% in inflation protected bonds (TIPS). This is slightly less risky than the basic portfolio above, but the return is almost the same. (I know, I know . . . it isn't terribly exciting yet, but don't get too worked up, wait for the rest of the changes.)

Step Two: Modify bonds

January 1970-December 2013

	Annualized Return	Annualized Standard Deviation
Step One: The basics	8.8%	11.3%
Step Two: Modify bonds	8.7%	10.9%

$100,000 grew to $3,849,488

Portfolio One	$4,069,110
Portfolio Two	$3,849,488
Difference	$(219,622)

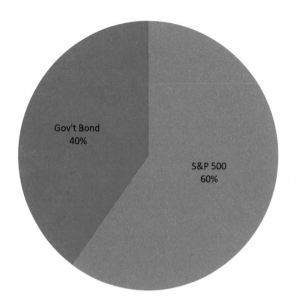

Step Three: Add Real Estate Index

Real estate investment trusts (REITs) have historically returned around 10% per year. **Conventional wisdom** holds real estate and stocks go well together because they do not always move in the same direction—they tend to help cancel out the risk of the other asset class.

So . . . after adding REITS to 20% of the stock part of this portfolio our returns are back to where we started, but the risk remains much lower. Again, still not earth shattering, but the best is yet to come.

conventional wisdom: beliefs generally accepted as true by the public or experts—in other words, what most people think

Step Three: Add real estate index

January 1970-December 2013

	Annualized Return	Annualized Standard Deviation
Step One: The basics	8.8%	11.3%
Step Two: Modify bonds	8.7%	10.9%
Step Three: Add REITs	8.8%	10.4%

$100,000 grew to $4,030,581

Portfolio One	$4,069,110
Portfolio Three	$4,030,581
Difference	$(38,529)

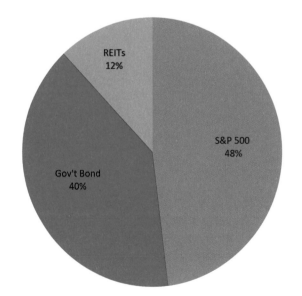

Step Four: Add Small Cap Stock Index

The portfolio shown in steps one and two consists mostly of the stocks of the five hundred largest U.S. companies—familiar names you might see in the news every day like ExxonMobil, General Electric, Johnson & Johnson, and PepsiCo. These companies did not start out huge though—at one point they were considered "small cap" companies. Because small companies can grow much faster than large ones, a basic diversification technique is to invest in stocks of small companies—that's step four. Notice that the portfolio now has an annualized return of 8.9%, with a standard deviation of 10.8%—so far this strategy has added about $265,000 to the cumulative return with lower risk.

Step Four: Add small cap stock index

January 1970-December 2013

	Annualized Return	Annualized Standard Deviation
Step One: The basics	8.8%	11.3%
Step Two: Modify bonds	8.7%	10.9%
Step Three: Add REITs	8.8%	10.4%
Step Four: Add small cap	8.9%	10.8%

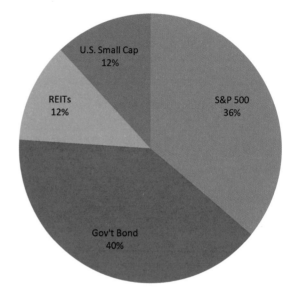

$100,000 grew to $4,334,554

Portfolio One	$4,069,110
Portfolio Four	$4,334,554
Difference	$265,444

Step Five: Add Value Stock Indexes

Growth stocks are those with rising sales and profits that investors expect to do well because of growth potential—these already make up the bulk of the S&P 500 Index. Value stocks are those that are simply "on sale" because investors believe the company is having one kind of issue or another that it is solving. So, in this example, let's add large company value and small company value indexes. The risk is still lower than the last step, but returns have gone way up!

Step Five: Add value stock indexes

January 1970-December 2013

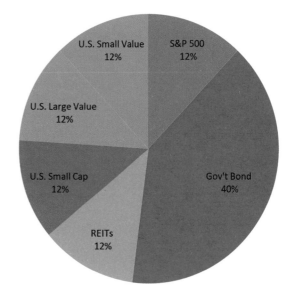

	Annualized Return	Annualized Standard Deviation
Step One: The basics	8.8%	11.3%
Step Two: Modify bonds	8.7%	10.9%
Step Three: Add REITs	8.8%	10.4%
Step Four: Add small cap	8.9%	10.8%
Step Five: Add value	9.9%	10.7%

$100,000 grew to $6,471,301

Portfolio One	$4,069,110
Portfolio Five	$6,471,301
Difference	$2,402,191

Step Six: Add International Indexes

In this last step, we are going to add additional indexes that include international stocks and emerging market stocks.

Now let's put it all together . . .

Our starting point was a return 8.8%, with a standard deviation of 11.3%. After six well thought out steps to diversify, the portfolio now has returns of 10.5% with a standard deviation of 11.2%.

Over the 44-year period shown, this portfolio would have grown to almost $8.2 million, twice as much as the traditional model shown in Step One—with less risk!

Step Six: Go global

January 1970-December 2013

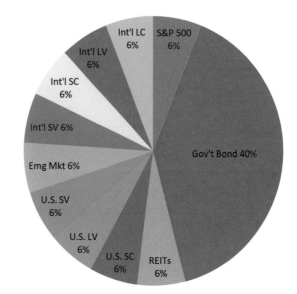

	Annualized Return	Annualized Standard Deviation
Step One: The basics	8.8%	11.3%
Step Two: Modify bonds	8.7%	10.9%
Step Three: Add REITs	8.8%	10.4%
Step Four: Add small cap	8.9%	10.8%
Step Five: Add value	9.9%	10.7%
Step Six: Go global	10.5%	11.2%

$100,000 grew to $8,164,368

Portfolio One	$4,069,110
Portfolio Six	$8,164,368
Difference	$4,095,258

TAKEAWAY #12:

Don't put all your eggs in one basket. Stay diversified and follow a plan.

CHAPTER 7

PUTTING IT ALL TO WORK—WHERE DO I ACTUALLY INVEST?

How Do I Invest, Where Do I Put My Money, and Do I Need More Advice?

So, all the information in this book may be great, but you may be asking what good it does you if you don't even know where to start investing. What other advice do you need? That's what this chapter is for.

Before you start working or actually even earn any income, your only real option for investing whatever money you may have is to invest in a regular investment account. By "regular" I mean one that is taxed normally by our government without any special rules. Open a magazine, look online, watch TV and you will see all sorts of advertisements for brokerage firms and banks. TD Ameritrade, E*Trade, Fidelity, Vanguard, Charles Schwab—just to name a very few. It's as simple as going online or calling and opening a regular taxable account and depositing your money.

And while they all offer different mutual funds and ETFs, different fee structures and different investing platforms, they all serve the same purpose: to provide an account for you to invest money. After you've researched and decided which brokerage shop is the best for you, open an account by filling out an application, decide what investments you want, deposit your funds and place your trade. It really is that easy. Hopefully after reading this book, you are convinced that it should be a low-cost and passive ETF.

But it gets a bit more complicated once you start earning money or have a job that offers retirement investment options.

If you don't work for a company that offers a formal retirement plan of any sort, you should consider an **IRA**. IRA's are creatures of our tax code and the federal government, and the rules surrounding them are mostly governed by the tax man (the IRS and its rules). The main difference between a regular taxable account and an IRA is that an IRA provides certain tax benefits that regular accounts do not.

IRA: an "income retirement account"

You can elect, instead, to invest in a different type of retirement account that is sponsored by your employer, if that is available to you. A **401k** is a retirement plan that allows you to set aside money directly from your paycheck to be invested. All of these plans are fairly similar, but these employee-sponsored plans may give you free money. True statement. Some employers will match some or all of the money you invest in these retirement plans. If you are lucky enough to work for a company that offers a match, then absolutely, unequivocally, you should take advantage and at least contribute the amount to get the full employer match. Literally, it's free money.

> If you happen to work for the government or a non-profit organization, then you may be offered a 403b or a 457 plan instead of a 401k.

DID YOU KNOW?

The difference between a Roth retirement account and a traditional retirement account (401k, IRA, etc.) is how each is taxed. Contributions to traditional retirement accounts are tax-deductible in the year the funds are contributed. But in exchange for that early tax break, all gains on the investment are taxed decades later once the funds are withdrawn. Contributions to Roth retirement accounts, on the other hand, are fully taxed in the year the contributions were made, but the investment grows tax free.

So traditional IRAs, for example, get an immediate tax break, whereas Roth IRAs can be withdrawn without paying taxes later. There are other subtleties between the two (you wouldn't expect our tax code to be simple, would you?), but the decision between them is based on what you think tax rates will look like in the future (good luck) and what you think your tax bracket will be in the future. If you are certain that tax rates (or your specific tax rate) will be higher in the future, then you should lean towards a Roth account, and vice versa.

So, you may ask, why wouldn't I just put all my money in, say, my company's 401k if I get the free-money-employer-match? Well, that should likely be your first retirement option. Unfortunately, there are limits on the amount of funds you can contribute to each plan—and some of those limits are based on how much money you make.

Another option your employer may offer, a health savings account (an HSA), is a tax-exempt account that is used with certain health insurance plans. Why, you ask, would this savings and investing book include a discussion on HSAs and health insurance? Assuming your employer offers a high-deductible health plan (the only plan that can be partnered with an HSA), then it's the single best retirement vehicle around. Contributions to HSAs must be used to pay for health and medical expenses, but they don't have to be used in the same year and can be left to grow for years or even decades.

Why is this the best retirement account? Well, it is a super-charged, tax-efficient vehicle. Contributions are immediately tax deductible. Growth is tax free. Withdrawals are tax free. It's sort of like a Roth account and a traditional account got married and had a baby—the HSA combines the best of each. But, again, the amount you can contribute each year is limited, so you'll still have to use other savings options.

At some point in your working career, after a few jobs and after your income (hopefully) increases, you'll wake up one day with several accounts, and multiple types of different accounts. Traditional, Roth, IRA, 401k, HSA, previous employer's 401k, etc. Accounts from prior employers can be combined and "rolled over" into one account at a large brokerage firm, but you may have several of these types of retirement accounts. And, there are yet more types of accounts if you work in the public sector or are self-employed (pensions, Thrift Savings Plans, SEP IRAs, Simple IRAs, Solo 401k, etc.).

> **FUN FACT!**
>
> *A "target date fund" is a pool of investments that are tailored to an investor's age and goals—the types of investments (its asset allocation) are altered each year so that the individual doesn't have to manage the investment. For example, if you are twenty, and think you'll retire at sixty, then you invest in a target retirement date fund for forty years, and the asset allocation automatically becomes more conservative over time for those forty years. A target date fund for someone with a thirty-year retirement would start with a more conservative mix than a forty-year horizon. Set-it-and-forget-it, so to speak. Many 401k plans allow the employee to default to a target date fund based on their age.*

How About Financial Advisors—Are They Worth It?

Why ask this question? Because financial advisors (FAs) customarily charge 1–1.5% per year on the total value of the investment portfolio. But studies have shown that utilizing a FA has the potential to add up to 3% annually to your returns—that is quite a significant improvement from investing alone! But after diving into the findings, here is what you'll find:

- Half of that 3% is simply the advisor calming clients in market swings or through emotional investing times—so, if you simply stick to your long-term investment horizon, ignore the hype and don't watch the news, then there is no need to pay someone to tell you that!
- Another 0.75% was attributable to an advisor setting forth a sensible asset allocation—again, if you're accumulating wealth for the long-term, simply look to a portfolio similar to what is presented in Chapter 6 and the work is done for you!
- And finally, most of the remainder of the added value from hiring an advisor is attributable to them simply guiding clients into low-cost investments—hopefully you're already convinced of this after reading Chapter 5.

Also know that many FAs receive fees when their clients invest in certain investments. So, some FAs get paid to recommend investments which may not be the best for you—that is a conflict of interest (be careful!).

When Should You Consider Hiring an Advisor?

There are certainly instances when a professional advisor's guidance is needed. A very few examples when their advice can be worth the cost: when to take legally required minimum distributions (RMDs) from your retirement accounts, tax issues, assistance with financial planning related to your estate plan (for example, setting up a will), or if you are unsure what types of insurance to purchase. But if you are young; in the long-term wealth accumulation stage of your life; and utilizing passive, low cost, diversified ETFs, there is likely not a reason to spend your money on a FA.

If you have decided that you do need a FA to assist you with certain life events or planning, then pay a FA on an hourly basis only, and only when you need the specific advice. There is simply no reason for most people to pay up to 1.5% on the value of their portfolio and pay that fee every year.

TAKEAWAY #13:
Only hire a professional financial advisor if you really need one— don't automatically assume you should hire one.

FUN FACT!
Are robots and artificial intelligence (AI) really taking over our lives? Self driving cars and trucks, jobs being automated, robotic soldiers . . . time will tell, but AI can take over some of our investing decisions. Meet robo-advisors—online portfolio managers that use complicated formulas and algorithms to automatically make investment decisions for you. These automated tools change asset allocation and make trades to save taxes, all at relatively low costs compared to FAs. So, if a full-fledged human FA is more than you need but you are not a do-it-yourself-type, then a robo-advisor may be a compromise to consider. And the fees are pretty reasonable also.

Emotional Investing Has Its Cost

We know that historical annual stock returns are around 8–9%. But, if you recall Takeaway #8 in Chapter 5, the average investor's annual return is only a pitiful 5%. That's because we are really terrible at investing. If we just sat tight and invested in low-cost, passive ETFs for the long haul we'd clip almost 9% per year. But we don't, because generally people have to "do" something—science has proven it.

> a pretty cool area of study called "behavioral finance" analyzes why people make dumb investing decisions

Studies show that if there is a story on the news about a particular stock, some people want to buy the stock and others want to sell—obviously they can't both be right! Emotional investing causes investors to knee-jerk into "doing" something when they should be investing for the long term. Some people are so scared of the market going down that at the slightest hint of bad news, they sell for no good reason except fear. And people's fear of missing out ("FOMO") causes a herd mentality, and investors buy stock just because others are buying—not for any other reason. We are overconfident. We overreact. We make emotional investment decisions. And every time this occurs, investors are paying fees and commissions. Add all this up, and emotional investing means you earn just 5% annual returns. So again, people are terrible investors.

> when people sell out of fear it is called "myopic loss aversion"

Remember from Chapter 5 what happens if you try to time the market? Miss the ten best days over the twenty-year period that ended after 2017 and your average annual return was just 3.5%; miss the thirty best days you would have lost money.

TAKEAWAY #14:
You are a terrible investor—remember that you can't beat the market. Buy low cost ETFs and ignore all the hype and news.

FINAL EXAM QUESTIONS

(BY THE WAY, NONE OF THESE IS A TRICK QUESTION)

1) Suppose you had $100 in a savings account and the interest rate was 2% per year. After five years, how much do you think you would have in the account if you left the money to grow?

    A. More than $102   B. Exactly $102   C. Less than $102

2) Imagine that the interest rate on your savings account was 1% per year and inflation was 2% per year. After one year, which of the following is correct?

    A. You would be able to buy more than today with the money in the account.
    B. You would be able to buy exactly the same as the money in the account today.
    C. You would be able to buy less than today with the money in the account.

3) Buying a single company stock usually provides a safer return than a stock mutual fund?

    A. True   B. False

DON'T READ THIS PARAGRAPH UNTIL YOU HAVE ANSWERED THE QUESTIONS!

I didn't make up these questions–they were developed by experts in the field of financial research and have been used in surveys and studies to determine the financial literacy of American adults. And the results might shock you: only 34% of adults over the age of 50 got all three questions correct. 67% got question #1 correct; 75% got question #2 correct; and 52% got question #3 correct. The answers: 1 - a; 2 - c; 3 - false.

CHAPTER 8
MONEY IS NOT EVERYTHING

The Parable of the Mexican Fisherman and the Banker

An American banker was taking a much-needed vacation in a small coastal Mexican village when a small boat with just one fisherman docked. The boat had several large, fresh fish in it. The investment banker was impressed and asked the Mexican how long it took to catch them.

The Mexican replied, "Only a little while." The banker then asked why he didn't stay out longer and catch more fish? The Mexican fisherman replied he had enough to support his family's immediate needs.

The American then asked, "But what do you do with the rest of your time?" The Mexican fisherman replied, "I sleep late, fish a little, play with my children, take a siesta with my wife, stroll into the village each evening, sip wine, and play guitar with my amigos: I have a full and busy life, señor."

The investment banker scoffed, "I work on Wall Street, and I could help you. You could spend more time fishing and with the proceeds buy a bigger boat, and with the proceeds from the bigger boat you could buy several boats until eventually you would have a whole fleet of fishing boats. Instead of selling your catch to the middleman you could sell directly to the processor, eventually opening your own cannery. You could control the product, processing, and distribution."

Then he added, "Of course, you would need to leave this small coastal fishing village and move to Mexico City or New York or Los Angeles where you would run your growing enterprise." The Mexican fisherman asked, "But señor, how long will this all take?" To which the American replied, "Fifteen to twenty years."

"But what then?" asked the fisherman. The banker laughed and said, "That's the best part. When the time is right you sell your company and become very rich. You could make millions."

"Millions, señor? Then what?"

To which the investment banker replied, "Then you would retire. You could move to a small coastal fishing village where you would sleep late, fish a little, play with your kids, take a siesta with your wife, stroll to the village in the evenings, sip wine, and play your guitar with your amigos."

TAKEAWAY #15:
While you should absolutely plan for the future, don't lose sight of the present. Enjoy your life now. It's not all about money.

Life is Short—Enjoy What You Do (That May Just Lead to Riches Anyway)

Life is too short to waste on doing something that you don't love. You can do anything you want for your career, so make sure you are passionate about it. Don't waste your opportunities simply sitting behind a desk all day because you think that is the path to riches. You do not have to choose between happiness and money—you can have both.

In fact, there was a study done in the 1960s in which graduating college seniors were asked to choose between one of the following:

A.   Find a job where they thought they could make the most money to invest, or
B.   Do what they were passionate about and hope the money follows.

Fifteen hundred students participated in this study. Twenty years later, a total of eighty-three had become millionaires. Of the eighty-three millionaires, only a few came from group A. Almost all of the millionaires came from group B! The takeaway of this study is simple: if you do what you love, the riches may follow. Odds are, if you just pursue the money, you may not be happy and might end up miserable.

More than likely, if you pursue your passion you will end up making a lot more money anyway because you'll love what you're doing.

TAKEAWAY #16:
Pursue your passion and curiosity rather than money— odds are you'll end up both happy and financially secure anyway.

TAKEAWAYS

(YES, AGAIN. BECAUSE THEY ARE IMPORTANT!)

1. Start saving early; let compounding work wonders for you!

2. Pay credit card debt every month in full.

3. Set goals; make a budget and stick to it.

4. Everything is negotiable.

5. Find out what is important to the other person—ask "why" questions.

6. Invest your money in safe investments if you do not have a lot of time to make your money back or if you need the cash quickly. Take more risk (for higher reward) for longer term savings goals.

7. Invest in indexes; don't be a fool and try to beat the market!

8. Do not try to time the market—you can't! Buy and hold is the best long-term strategy.

9. Do not chase returns!

10. The market always reverts to the mean.

11. Minimize expenses, invest in low-cost index funds.

12. Don't put all your eggs in one basket. Stay diversified and follow a plan.

13. Only hire a professional financial advisor if you really need one—don't automatically assume you should hire one.

14. You are a terrible investor—remember that you can't beat the market. Buy low cost ETFs and ignore all the hype and news.

15. While you should absolutely plan for the future, don't lose sight of the present. Enjoy your life now. It's not all about money.

16. Pursue your passion and curiosity rather than money—odds are you'll end up both happy and financially secure anyway.

SOURCES AND CREDITS

Chapter 1: Savings

- Holden, Karen et al., working paper No. 2009-009, "Financial Literacy Programs Targeted on Pre-School Children: Development and Evaluation." La Follette School of Public Affairs at the University of Wisconsin-Madison, 2009.
- Organisation for Economic Co-operation and Development (OECD; The World Bank).
- Consumer Federation of America and the Financial Planning Association, 2006.
- "Report on the Economic Well-Being of U.S. Households." The Federal Reserve Board, July 2014.

Chapter 2: Budgeting, Debt, and Setting Goals

- U.S. Department of the Treasury, Bureau of the Public Debt.
- Federal Reserve.
- Consumer Finance Protection Bureau.
- Administrative Office of the U.S. Courts.
- U.S. Department of Education's National Center for Education Statistics (NCES).
- U.S. Census Bureau.
- U.S. Department of Education, National Center for Education Statistics, "Annual Earnings of Young Adults" in "The Condition of Education 2014" (NCES 2014-083). May 2014.
- Dr. Gail Matthews, Dominican University of California.

Chapter 5: Active v. Passive—Which Is Better?

- S&P Indices Versus Active Funds (SPIVA) Scorecard, Year-End 2017, percentages rounded, indices referenced: Large Cap (S&P 500), Mid Cap (S&P Midcap 400), Small Cap (S&P Small Cap 600), Int'l (S&P 700), Emerging Market (S&P/IFCI Composite), Real Estate (S&P BMI U.S. REIT).
- Dalbar, Inc. Quantitative Analysis of Investor Behavior, 2019.
- Morningstar, "2018 Fundamentals for Investors". 2018.
- Davis Advisors.

- Callan Associates, Inc. "Callan Periodic Table of Investment Returns." 2018.
- "Principle 3: Minimize cost." https://personal.vanguard.com/us/insights/investingtruths/investing-truth-about-cost.

Chapter 6: Diversification

- **The six step "process" shown is merely one example of a well-diversified portfolio.** Portions of the original "Ultimate Buy and Hold Strategy" by Paul Merriman and Rich Buck have been reprinted with permission. For the full version, and other Merriman insights, please see http://paulmerriman.com/the-ultimate-buy-hold-strategy-2014/.
- Final exam questions from Annamaria Lusardi and Olivia Mitchell, U.S. Health and Retirement Study on financial literacy.

Chapter 7: Putting It All to Work—Where Do I Actually Invest?

- Kinniry Jr., Francis M., Colleen M. Jaconetti, Michael A. DiJoseph, Yan Zilbering and Donald G. Bennyhoff. "Putting a Value on Your Value: Quantifying Vanguard Advisor's Alpha." Vanguard, 2016.
- Dalbar, Inc. "Quantitative Analysis of Investor Behavior." 2019.

Chapter 8: Money Is Not Everything

- Blotnick, Srully. *Getting Rich Your Own Way*. 1982.

INDEX

WORKSHEETS AND ACTIVITIES

Saving & Investing Worksheet

1) Use the "Rule of 72" to approximate the following:

• $1,000 initial investment, at a 6% average annual return. What is the value after 36 years?
    A. $4,000   B. $6,000   C. $13,000   D. $8,000

• $1,000 initial investment, at a 12% average annual return. What is the value after 36 years?
    A. $13,000   C. $64,000   C. $128,000   D. $48,000

2) What is inflation? Describe how it affects purchasing power.

_____
_____
_____
_____

3) Explain why hyper-inflation and deflation both have negative effects on economies.

_____
_____
_____
_____

4) What are the differences between "wants" and "needs"? Provide examples of each.

_____
_____
_____
_____

5) Using the risk spectrum below, place these investment options in order of least risky to most risky.

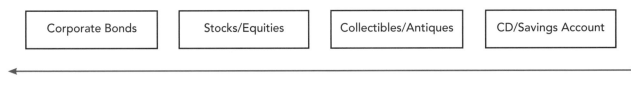

| Corporate Bonds | Stocks/Equities | Collectibles/Antiques | CD/Savings Account |

Less risk   More risk

6) True or False: Past investment returns provide an accurate indication of future performance of an investment.
    A. True   B. False

7) Circle whether the identified investment is an appropriate investment for a long- or short-term investment horizon.
- Cash   Long term / Short term
- Certificate of Deposit/Savings Account   Long term / Short term
- Antiques/Collectibles   Long term / Short term
- Real Estate   Long term / Short term
- U.S. Government Treasury Bills   Long term / Short term
- Foreign Equities   Long term / Short term
- Investment Grade Corporate Debentures   Long term / Short term

8) True or False: Actively managed funds are more likely to beat their benchmark than passive funds.
    A. True   B. False

9) Circle the correct answer: Diversifying investments increases or decreases risk compared to a single investment?
    A. Increase   B. Decrease

10) The average investor's return is far lower than the market average return because of which of the following? Circle all that apply.
    A. People invest irrationally based on emotion.   B. Investors try to time the market.
    C. Frequent trading results in more commissions   D. Investors chase returns.

11) True or False: Lower costs/expenses are the best indicator of the future performance of a fund.

    A. True   B. False

12) True or False: Passively managed funds or ETFs generally have higher costs/expenses than their actively managed counterparts.

    A. True   B. False

13) Which of the following is the most diversified portfolio?

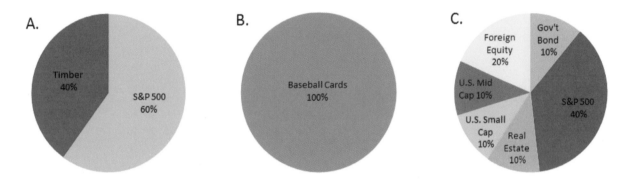

14) You should aim to save at least what percent of your income?

    A. 78%   B. 6%   C. 3%   D. 15%

15) Research project: On a separate sheet of paper, explain how either of the following concepts can negatively affect investing behavior: "myopic loss aversion" or "social validation."

Saving & Investing Crossword

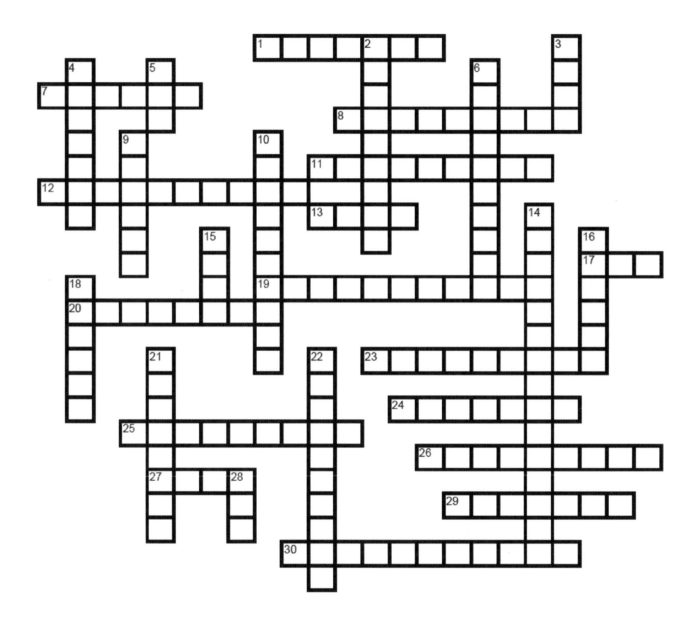

ACROSS

1. Investment style that mimics an index or matches a benchmark
7. Document setting forth income and spending used for planning
8. Standard used to measure performance of an investment
11. General decrease in the prices of goods
12. Investment vehicle comprised of securities using funds pooled from many investors
13. Debt investment wherein one party lends money to another
17. An index fund that trades like a security (abbreviation)
19. Past _____ does not guarantee future results
20. Money paid for the use of money or delaying debt repayment
23. General increase in the prices of goods
24. Amount that expenses exceed revenues; loss
25. _____ to mean. Markets always generate their historical average returns.
26. Dollar cost _____: making constant scheduled purchases of the same amount in a security
27. Government entity that insures bank deposits (abbreviation)
29. Investment _____: anticipated length of hold time of an investment
30. Adding earnings to an initial investment that also earns money

DOWN

2. Type of mutual fund that tracks a benchmark or index
3. The possibility of losses compared with the probability of expected return on an investment
4. Amount that revenues exceed expenses; profit
5. Government watchdog entity for investments and securities (abbreviation)
6. A fee charged to an investor by a broker to trade a security
9. Ownership in an asset
10. Legal procedure involving an entity unable to pay debts
14. Spreading investments in different securities/asset classes
15. Payment to an employee based on hours or days worked
16. Amount earned on an investment, expressed as a percentage
18. Able to be easily and quickly converted into cash
21. Quick method used to determine when money doubles, based on the annual return
22. Asset _____: how one divides investments among different asset classes

Saving Goals Worksheet

As you read this you know that you may have to wait before you can buy something you want because you don't have the money. There is a difference between things you want and things you need.

And we all have to make choices about how to spend our money. This is called budgeting. A budget sets forth your anticipated income and spending over a period of time. It allows you to see what you can afford, how much you can spend, and if you need to cut back on buying things because you don't (or won't) have enough money.

There is simply not enough money to buy everything you might want. You must prioritize . . . you may have to wait to buy something you want because you can't afford it or because you need something else. Before you buy something, research it, shop around, compare prices, and ask questions. Do you really need the item, or can you live without it? Are you replacing something broken? Do you have something else that will work just as well? What advantages does the new one offer?

Once you have made decisions about what you are going to purchase you can then set savings goals for those items. In fact, studies have shown that people who actually write down their goals on a piece of paper are 33% more likely to reach them. Use this worksheet to help you reach your savings goals.

Goal	Cost	Number of Months Until Purchase	Monthly Savings Needed	Weekly Savings Needed

ANSWER KEYS

Saving & Investing Worksheet Answer Key

1. D; B

2. Inflation is the general increase in the price of goods and services. Inflation has the effect of lowering the purchasing power of money which does not increase in value at the same rate of inflation.

3. Hyper-inflation causes goods and services to increase at a much higher rate than wages, eroding the purchasing power of money. This effectively causes people to feel poorer and they stop buying goods and services. Deflation results in goods that people might purchase being worth less the next day, and even less the day after, etc. This makes consumers less willing to spend money, the negative effect of which is noticed on the economy as a whole.

4. Needs are items that are necessary in order to live one's life—like food, clothes, shelter, etc. Wants are those items that make people happier but are not necessary to healthy and safe living. Examples of wants include cell phones, expensive name brand clothes, fancy shoes, video games, entertainment, etc.

5. CD / SAVINGS . . . CORPORATE BOND . . . STOCKS / EQUITIES . . . COLLECTIBLES /ANTIQUES

6. FALSE

7. Cash   Short term

8. Certificate of Deposit/Savings Account   Short term

9. Antiques/Collectibles   Long term

10. Real Estate   Long term

11. U.S. Government Treasury Bills   Short term

12. Foreign Equities   Long term

13. Investment Grade Corporate Debentures   Short term

14. FALSE

15. DECREASE

16. ALL ANSWERS ARE ACCURATE

17. TRUE

18. FALSE

19. C

20. D

21. "Myopic loss aversion" occurs when investors temporarily lose sight of their long-term goals and focus on potential immediate losses. The body/mind experience the same physiological response as "fight or flight" syndrome. This results in panicked, irrational selling based on emotion. "Social validation" is our innate desire to be a part of the crowd. It causes a perceived validation of investment decisions by following the herd and doing what others are doing, without any sound investment rationale.

Saving & Investing Crossword Answer Key

ACROSS
1. PASSIVE
7. BUDGET
8. BENCHMARK
11. DEFLATION
12. MUTUAL FUND
13. BOND
17. ETF
19. PERFORMANCE
20. INTEREST
23. INFLATION

24. DEFICIT
25. REVERSION
26. AVERAGING
27. FDIC
29. HORIZON
30. COMPOUNDING

DOWN
2. INDEX FUND
3. RISK
4. SURPLUS

5. SEC
6. COMMISSION
9. EQUITY
10. BANKRUPTCY
14. DIVERSIFICATION
15. WAGE
16. RETURN
18. LIQUIDITY
21. RULE OF 72
22. ALLOCATION
28. CPI